The Presenter's EZ Graphics Kit

The Presenter's EZ Graphics Kit

A Step by Step Guide for the Artistically Challenged to Creating Original and Effective Lettering, Borders, Visuals and Images for Flip Charts, Overheads, and Presentation Software

Second Edition

By Lori Backer and Michele Deck

STERLING, VIRGINIA

Published in 2003 by

Stylus Publishing, LLC
22883 Quicksilver Drive
Sterling, Virginia 20166

Library of Congress Cataloging-in-Publication-Data
Backer, Lori.
  The presenter's EZ graphics kit : a step by step guide for the artistically challenged to creating original and effective lettering, borders, visuals, and images for flip charts, overheads, and presentation software / by Lori Backer and Michele Deck.-- 2nd ed.
        p. cm.
  ISBN 1-57922-071-1 (pbk. plus CD-ROM : alk. paper)
1. Business presentations--Graphic methods. I. Deck, Michele L. II. Title.   HF5718.22.B32 2003
741'.0285--dc21
                                2003005713

Second edition, 2003
ISBN: paperback 1-57922-071-1

Printed in the United States of America

All first editions printed on acid free paper

Many Thanks

There are so many very special people in our lives who give of their ideas, creativity and spirit so generously. We have each had many mentors, friends and relatives we are grateful to.

John von Knorring, who is a forward thinker and innovator in the publishing world.

Barb Watts, who worked tirelessly to make our first endeavor a successful one.

All of the **training and teaching associates** we have met in our many travels over the last 13 years who have offered pearls of wisdom to us.

Brett Williams who is our high technology wizard and the very best "E-Guy" we know.

Brian, Brittany, Melanie and Melissa Deck who always support and encourage, while amazing Michele with their creative, caring and determined personalities.

Steven, Koby, TJ and Addy Backer who love and inspire Lori's artistic right brain.

 **Lynn Solem**, who not only inspired us but gave us each a very long and beautiful pearl necklace of wisdom. We love you and miss you.

And to all of you who feel artistically reluctant and challenged and yet seek to increase your ability to communicate visually, we would like to offer you special encouragement and congratulations.

Licensing Agreement

Please read this document as carefully as you would any legal document. If you determine that you cannot abide by the conditions of this licensing agreement, you may return *The Presenter's EZ Graphics Kit* with proof of purchase to Stylus Publishing within seven (7) days for a full refund.

1. Copyright. *The Presenter's EZ Graphics Kit,* including both the book and the attached CD-ROM, contains illustrations that are provided under license. *The Presenter's EZ Graphics Kit* is copyrighted by Stylus Publishing.

2. License. Stylus Publishing, LLC grants to the purchaser a non-exclusive license to use the illustrations in accordance with the terms of this license.

3. Copying, Photocopying and Reproducing Illustrations. The illustrations printed in the book and incorporated in the accompanying CD-ROM may be reproduced by hand, photocopied, copied onto overhead projection film and incorporated in computer presentation software by the purchaser or owner of the printed book. The printed illustrations and CD-ROM images may be used or adapted by the purchaser or be reproduced by hand by the purchaser's students. However the illustrations and images may only be used on one computer or projection system at a time. Site licenses can be obtained for an additional fee by contacting Stylus Publishing, LLC.

4. Transfer of Ownership. If ownership of a copy of *The Presenter's EZ Graphics Kit* should be transferred from one person to another, the person who gains ownership is also bound by this agreement.

5. Termination of Rights. If any portions of this licensing agreement are not adhered to, Stylus Publishing, LLC reserves the right to terminate this licensing agreement and seek legal remedy, including but not limited to financial damages and punitive fines.

Contents

Reasons To Use This Book!

Why Teach With Graphics?

According to the Gallup organization, in the year 2002, over 99.9% of US households owned some form of visual electronic technology - televisions, DVDs, VCRs. Consequently, the natural and easy communication styles of individuals have now shifted to a format that requires both visual and entertaining elements.

As a teacher or presenter, one of the fastest and easiest ways to reach an audience is with pictures, graphics and visual media. Believe it or not, an effective visual is *not* a computer generated screen with typed words projected before a group of people. Typed words are not visuals, and projected notes or words in a larger format so the audience can "read" along, do not engage the whole brain. Pictures and graphics that are tied to key words actually complete the process of communication in a way nothing else can.

Today's X/Y Generations dislike lectures, expect to be actively involved in the learning process and look for both high tech media (computer generated screens, slides, video) and low tech (transparencies, flip charts, posters) to aid their learning and retention.

What's A Good Graphic & When Should I Use Them?

 A good graphic is one that gets the message across in a simple, direct way. It grabs the attention of viewers and provokes their curiosity. It offers a link between learners' existing knowledge and/or their experience in a manner that invites the whole brain to be involved. When these links are established, retention is built in a learners' mind.

Graphics are used to teach or train *"need to know"* content and skills. They build a skeleton of knowledge that can be filled in with great detail. Visuals can break up large blocks of content into manageable chunks for learners. Graphics can refocus an audience at intervals by depicting concepts, and introducing critical points or humor.

Visuals can be used to deliver information, such as where rest facilities are located or when a lunch break will take place. Pictures can serve as reminders to turn cell phones to silent mode. They can be used to make any number of important points. With television generation learners in class, we cannot have too many visuals available for use as teaching and training tools.

What If I Can't Draw or I'm Artistically Challenged?

This book can change your perception of yourself as non-artistic. Whether you are looking for the ability to create dazzling power point slides or to simply illustrate your point on a flip chart, this book will teach you the elements of graphic design and usage that will develop your skills and also offer ways to improve them. We have also included Ready-to-Use samples that you can copy and personalize for your audience and your message.

What Do I Need to Remember about Using Graphics and Visuals?

Variety is the important thing to remember with graphic and visuals usage. Create different parts of your content on a variety of media and switch them at intervals. This will keep the attention of your audience and eliminate the "zoning out syndrome" that happens when people are seated in a darkened room for too long. A combination of high and low tech media can balance the need for technology with the more human side of teaching and learning.

How Can This Book Improve My Graphic Creating Abilities?

For many of us in the teaching, training and speaking professions, it is often necessary to communicate intangible ideas and concepts on the spot. We need to be able to think visually and communicate graphically often by drawing or creating images on demand.

This book shows you how to do just that by providing you with easy ways to get your point across using shapes, icons, and simple graphics to anchor thoughts in your audience memory.

You can copy, trace, duplicate, import or scan the icons, graphics, lettering and border examples directly from this book or the enclosed CD. Your artistic abilities will be enhanced and improved instantly.

Whether you choose a low or high tech medium to convey your key points, the ideas presented in this book are easy to copy and adapt.

You will also learn how to scan and save the art you create so that you can incorporate it in presentation software.

Start up Section
EZ Ways to Use this Book!

Book Sections

The Presenter's EZ Graphics Kit is divided into four main sections.

 1. Basics

 2. Graphics

 3. Quick & Easy

 4. Ready Mades

Each section contains examples that are designed to be traced, reduced, enlarged, reproduced and scanned so that you can start creating visuals immediately.

Section Guide

At the beginning of each section, look for the *EZ Guide* symbol. These opening pages offer you personal tips, ideas, witticisms and artistic encouragement.

EZ Guide also rates each section. The rating informs you about the extent of artistic challenge you will encounter and about preparation time considerations.

1. The Basics

The Basics section describes the process of good graphic design for any type of visual created. This section provides guidelines for creating and combining the basic foundation elements of a visual.

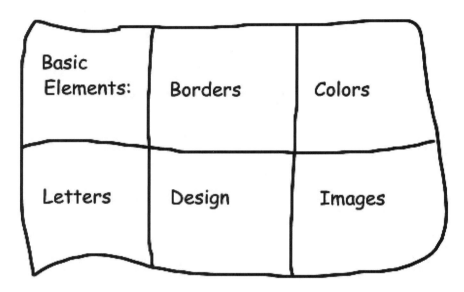

This section also suggests various color combinations that enhance retention. Step by step panels that demonstrate how to combine a variety of shapes to create unique images are included. Unique lettering styles and unusual visual borders are provided to make the visuals you create captivating.

EZ   Guide   Rating: Beginning foundations and warm up exercises. Preparation time: requires practice for proficiency.

2. The Graphics

Included in this section are step-by-step panels that show you how to combine simple shapes - circles, squares, lines - to create easy to draw graphics. You can create graphics quickly freehand or with computer drawing software by copying the various shape combinations shown in the panels. You can also copy and import directly from the CD.

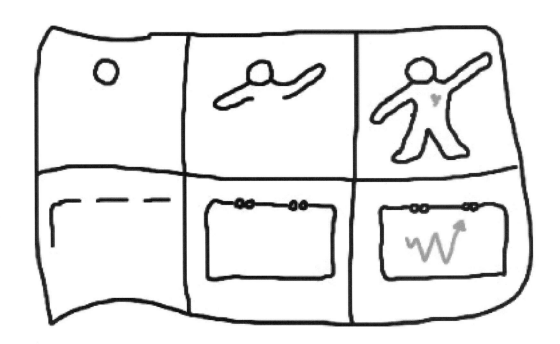

EZ Guide Rating:
Beginner-Intermediate.
Preparation time: practice copying shape combinations until you can draw the shape from memory.

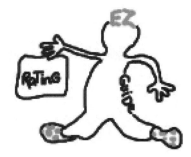

3. Quick and Easy Ideas

This section offers you some simple ideas you can use to create fun and informative visual agendas, graphic ways to display class logistical information, and ways to teach, review and reinforce information visually. There are suggestions for preserving, recycling and displaying your visuals and reproduction recommendations.

4. The Ready Mades

The Ready Mades are pre-prepared visuals ready for you to reproduce, enlarge, scan or personalize for use in your own teaching or training classes. A terrific resource for anyone who has to be ready to present without the luxury of prep time!

EZ Guide Rating:
Book mark these two sections. They are valuable resources for all artistic levels. And priceless for professionals with too much to do and not enough time.

5. The CD-ROM

Best use of the CD-ROM: For high tech users, browse through a variety of artistic ideas and choose the ones you want to import into your computer software. Possible software usages may include presentation software, internet course materials or course handouts, drawing software or desktop publishing software. And for easy, low technology graphic use, print out a graphic, enlarge it and attach it to a flip chart. Either way, use the graphic images on the CD-ROM as you would clip art sources.

All the graphics contained on the CD-ROM are provided in the JPEG format, and are placed in their respective folders as listed below. To use the graphics in a computer presentation, simply complete the following steps:

Select the graphic you want to use from the companion book.
Identify that graphic's file name.
Identify the folder where the graphic is located.
Insert and open the CD-ROM by following your computer's normal procedures.
Open the appropriate folder.
Insert the graphic into your presentation by following the graphic insertion procedures as prescribed in your presentation application.
Save your document.

The CD-ROM contains four sections of artwork:

1. **The Step-by-Step Graphic Panels**
   Locate the directory "step.by.step" on the CD-ROM. Inside of the directory the panels will be labeled with their respective name from the book.
2. **The Graphic Language Library**
   Locate the directory "graphic.library" on the CD-ROM. Inside of the directory the graphic files will have the name of the title below each picture from the book.
3. **The VIG (Very Important Graphics) Suprises**
   Locate the directory "vig" on the CD-ROM. Inside of the directory you will find graphics that will help you regain the attention of your audience by adding a touch of WOW!
4. **The Ready Made Visuals (Black and White)**
   Locate the directory "ready.made" on the CD-ROM. Inside of the directory the graphic files will be named according to their respective page number from the book.
5. **The Ready Made Visuals (Color)**
   Locate the directory "ready.made.color" on the CD-ROM. Inside of the directory the graphic files will be named according to their respective page number followed by a number denoting the color variation (ie 193.1.jpg or 193.2.jpg).

EZ Guide Rating:
You have everything on the CD-ROM, or after reading this book you have everything in your imagination. Just draw your creation and scan it directly into your computer, or presentation software.

Graphic Arts Check list

Materials to get started:

_____   Soft lead pencils
_____   Eraser

_____   Black, broad point fiber tipped drawing pens

_____   Large nibbed waterbased markers
_____   Small nibbed colored markers

_____   Drawing paper
_____   Tracing paper
_____   Sketch pads

_____   Straight edge ruler
_____   Paper clips
_____   Self sticking notes and tape flags

_____   Scotch brand invisible and masking tape for wall hanging

_____   Classical music (Optional)
_____   Chocolate chip cookies (Optional)

_____   **The Presenter's EZ Graphics Kit**
_____   **The EZ Graphics Kit CD-ROM**

 # The Basics

 Borders

Colors

Letters

 Design

Images

The Basics

 Borders

EZ Guide says: "Start with simple designs for your visuals -- use a large, eye-catching title, include a graphic image related to your message, place a sub-title towards the center and frame your idea with a double line border."

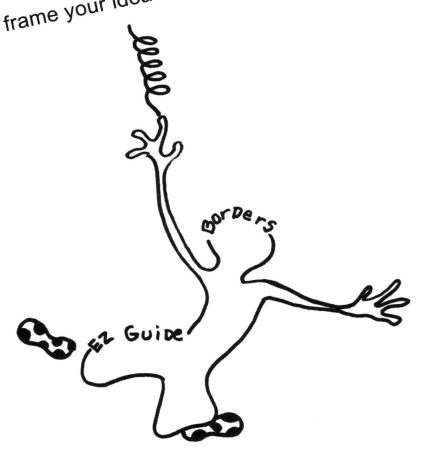

The Basics: Borders

The look of your visuals will appear more complete by placing a simple border around the content.

Borders act like frames for your ideas. A border is an easy technique that makes a big impact when used. It defines the layout space of your visual and gives it a completed, professional look.

Choose a border that encloses your information. It can be as simple as a lined box or as elaborate as your imagination can produce. Visual designers will often select a border that is related to their content, including a simple graphic or icon in the design.

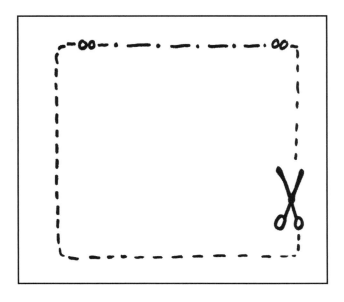

Allow your eyes to look back and forth between the two examples below. Which appeals to your eye more?

<table>
<tr>
<td>

FOR TITLES:

*Use capital letters
*Periodically vary size
*Use color codes to
indicate importance
*Check for unity of design

</td>
<td>

FOR TITLES:

```
graphic
```

*Use capital letters
*Periodically vary size
*Use color codes to
indicate importance
*Check for unity of design

</td>
</tr>
</table>

Your visuals will look more professional and complete if they contain a title in capital letters, usually in the upper third of the layout. The title can be in the same size print as the text, but we suggest it be in larger print.

Use bright, activating, major colors to make the title stand out. Once posted, your visual will be visually eye catching and appealing.

Creative Samples

Use words from your subject matter in your border. Alternate thick and thin letters along with dark and light colors.

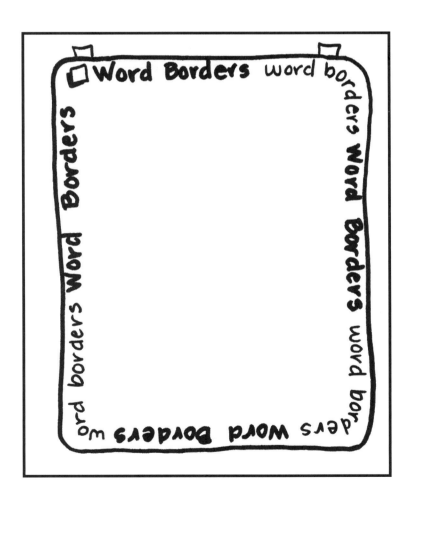

Line Borders

Vary the borders by using simple rounded lines. Add shaded areas for depth and contrast.

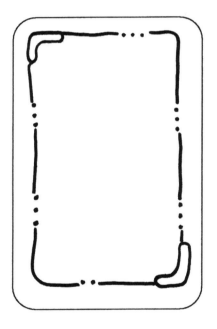 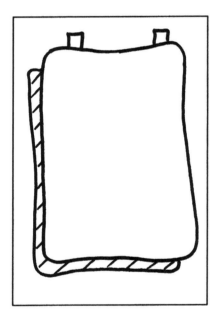

Graphic Samples

Use simple graphics and pictures for borders. Freehand the images, or use pictures and/or clip art for a different and unique effect.

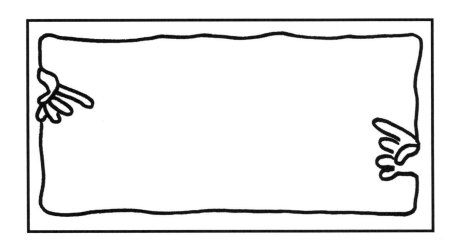

Computer Borders

TIME TO GEAR UP...

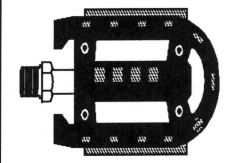

Shape up with Safety!

Border Samples

Border Samples

Border Practice Space

Border Practice Space

The Basics

Colors

EZ Guide says: "Catch your audience's attention quickly and then try to hang on to it by using three colors on your visuals."

Color can generate interest and can create excitement. Here are some guidelines:

Guide for **ACTIVATING** Colors

The following colors are considered extroverted colors, intense and emotion sparking. Note: you can see examples of color use in the accompanying CD-ROM

Red is a color that evokes strong emotion. It can empower, stimulate, dramatize and symbolize passion. It can also mean danger or disturbing information. It is good for highlighting important information, but not for extended text because, like purple, it is very tiring to the eye.

Orange represents feelings that are friendly, cheerful, energetic, and light feeling. It is the color that represents positive thinking, and can stimulate appetite and conversation. We do not recommend it for text but it is good for highlighting and bordering.

Yellow is the color of light and represents feelings of bright optimism. It stimulates and can invite creative thinking. It also inspires feelings of warmth and cheerfulness and can increase energy. Yellow is good for highlighting and coloring-in graphics.

Guide for **PACIFYING** Colors

The following colors are considered cool colors, calming and re-energizing.

Blue is a blending color. This color relaxes, refreshes and cools and can produce feelings of tranquility, calmness, trust and peace. It is good for letters, borders, graphics, and backgrounds.

Green is a friendly, healing color which represents growth, productivity and prosperity. This color refreshes, brings feelings of balance and encourages emotional growth. The darker shade of forest green is good for letters, borders and graphics.

Purple projects boldness, power and royalty. This color comforts, assures, creates mystery and draws out intuition. It is dense in nature and should not be used as often as the colors listed above. Dense colors can quickly tire the eyes. Purple is good for bold graphics, highlighting and borders.

Guide for **NEUTRALIZING** Colors

The following are actually non-colors. They neither activate nor pacify and are meant to be used as frames and to show off other colors.

Black represents the absence of color and can create emotions that strengthen and encourage independence. It is a good color for letters, borders, and graphics.

Brown is a warm earth tone color that projects feelings of strength, security and solidity. It is a stabilizing and supportive color and symbolizes the down-to-earth. It is good for letters, borders and graphics.

White is light. Use white space to lighten, expand, purify, energize, clean, unify, and enliven other colors. Use white space to present an uncluttered image and to give your visuals greater impact.

Guide for Highlighting Colors

Use activating colors to highlight, fill-in and shade. Avoid lettering with yellow, orange and light pink since these colors are difficult to see.

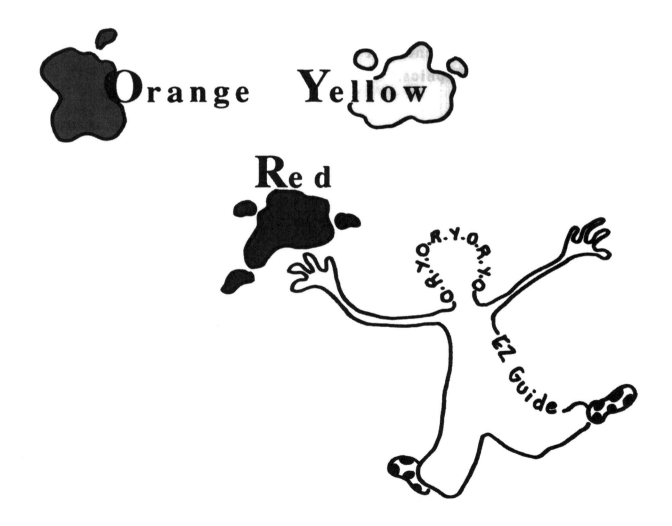

Guide for Using Major Colors

Use a maximum of **three** colors for your visuals, unless you are using a rainbow configuration of color. More than three major colors can fatigue the eye. The following are the major colors we recommend.

R e d

For titles, critical
words or phrases.

B l u e

For basic text,
graphics.

G r e e n

For non-critical
words, pictures.

B l a c k

An all-purpose
color good for
everything.

Rainbow Effect Example

Color Practice Space

Color Practice Space

 # The Basics

 Letters

EZ Guide says: "To provide variety, use one or two different styles of sizes or letters. With more than two styles, visuals can begin to look like ransom notes!"

Lettering varieties can add life and sparkle to any visual.
   If you need letters for flip charts, they can be generated on a
   computer and attached with invisible tape. There are automatic
   lettering machines that can generate letters as well. And there
   are times where you will want to create free-hand letters
   spontaneously.

Create letters one inch in height for every ten feet from the audience.
If the back of the group is twenty feet away from the visual, the letters
should be two inches and so on. Use a minimum of two inch tall or
larger letters on reusable flip charts.

Choose a style of lettering that suits and complements the message.
Using very large letters conveys a loud voice, while smaller letters
speak softly.

Lettering needs white space around it. This clarifies the message and helps it to stand out. Make sure that the layout of the letters is easy to read from a distance.

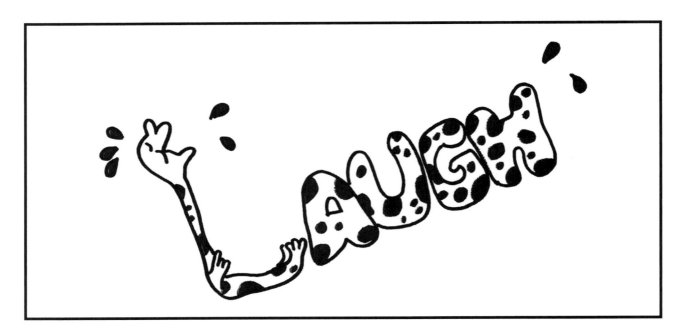

Letters can set the scene or create a mood by their shape or by the way they are decorated. Decorating the first letter in a word, sentence or paragraph is called illumination. Color can also add to the message and highlighting of the information. Some letters are designed to be a part of a picture, rather than being added above or below it.

The most important consideration about lettering is whether it conveys a clear message and if it is easy to read from a distance. If the message is long and complicated, use a simple style of lettering. Reserve excessively scrolled or fancy style letters for short messages or greetings as they are more difficult to read.

Provide visual contrast by coloring the background with a highlight color. Then place major color letters on top. If you use a pacifying color for the background, test that the lettering is easy to see.

When free-hand drawing, to add dimension and shadows to lettering, draw the basic structure first. Then, copy the outline a bit to one side, above or below the letter. Fill in the shadow with a darker color shade than the basic letter.

Headings should be presented in the largest letters in your visual. Use capitals for your header and lower case letters for the text, keeping the message short and clear. Leave adequate white space around illustrations or graphics.

Highlight, underline or enlarge key points, keeping letters evenly spaced.

Align letters evenly, when free-hand lettering, by using lined paper or by creating faint pencil lines called guidelines. The distance between letters should be even if you are creating uniform letters. Leave a space the size of a capital "E" between words made up of capital letters. Leave a space of a small "n" between words made up of small, lower case letters.

Each letter of the English alphabet has a basic shape. Letters can be printed free-standing or joined in an overlapping style. Free-standing letters are easier to read from a distance. Create a whole new alphabet to fit any theme. Thematic alphabets can be used in many ways, relating them to a special message.

Unique lettering styles create visuals that capture the eye's attention. Free-hand lettering on flip charts is easier to do with practice. We trace the letter style we like and then using a lettering grid pad(see next page), free-hand copy the traced letter, practicing several letters in a row.

It is often a good idea to warm-up and stretch the hands, fingers and wrists before drawing and lettering. The following exercises are for visual designers who will be preparing flip chart visuals free-hand. If you practice the wrist and hand warm-ups shown below before beginning, you will find it easier to create even letters and outstanding graphics.

Wrist and Hand Warm-Up

1. Hold arms out in front of you.

2. Bend arms at the elbow, pointing hands upward.

3. Keeping arms, wrists and hands relaxed, begin to gently twist, turn and rotate the hands.

4. Increase the speed of the wrist and hand rotations until the hands are twisting rapidly

5. Continue the rotations for two to three minutes

6. Bring arms down and relax before beginning to draw or letter.

Lettering Ideas

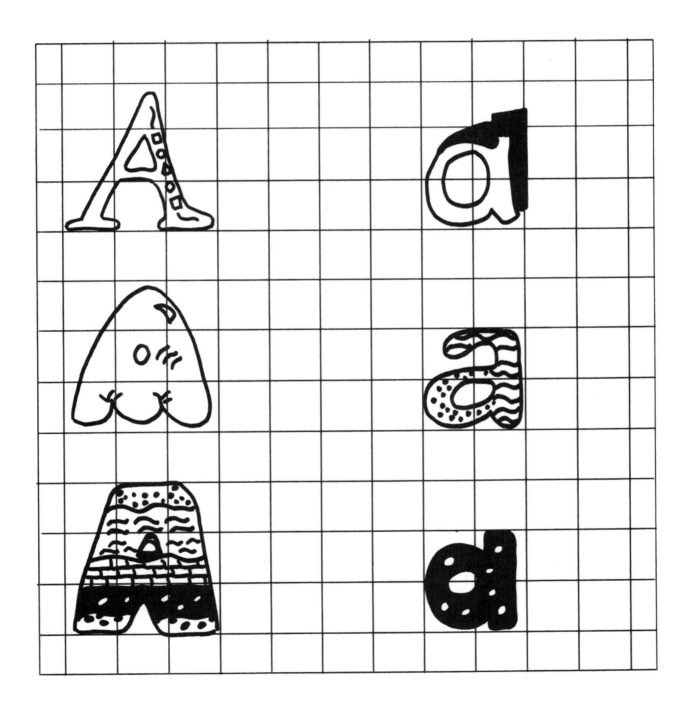

Lettering Ideas

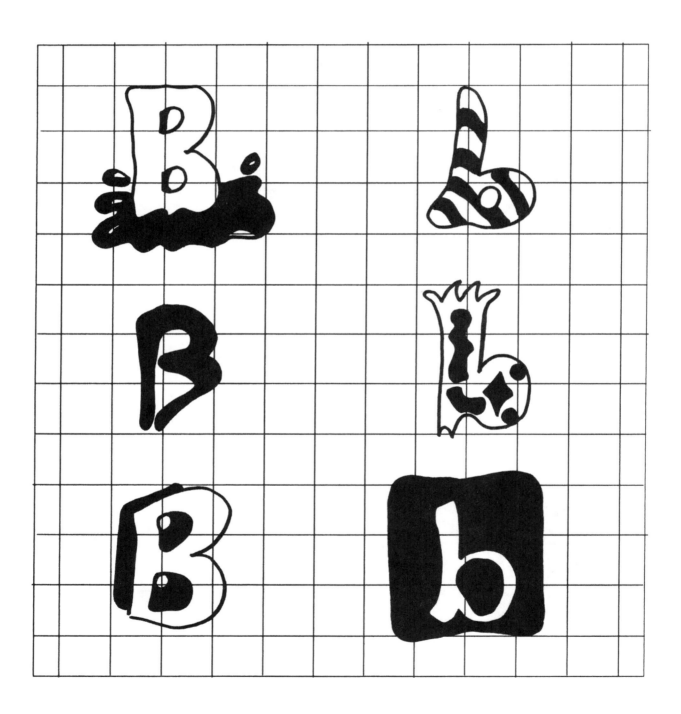

Lettering Ideas

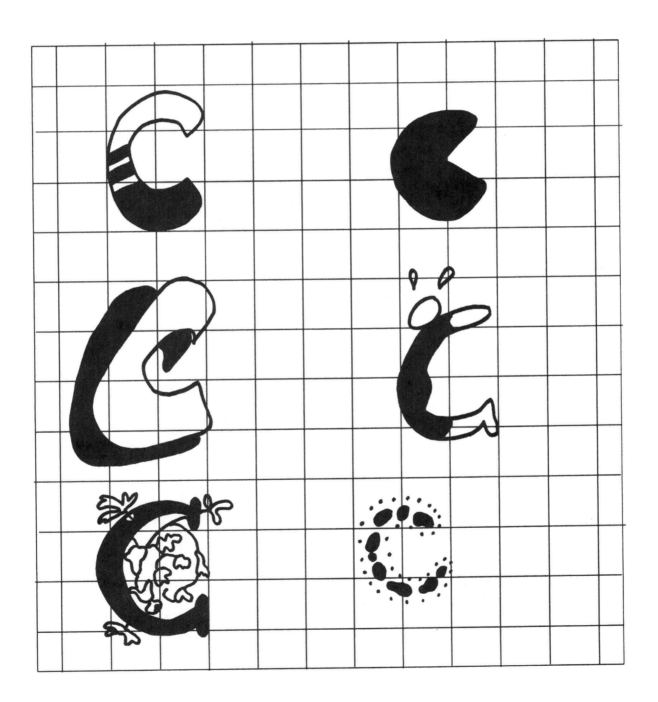

Lettering Ideas

Free Hand Alphabet

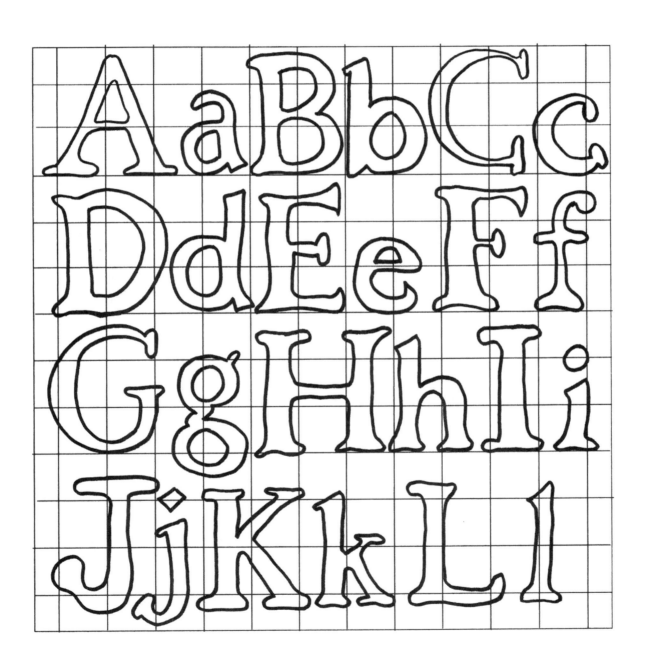

Free Hand Alphabet

Free Hand Alphabet

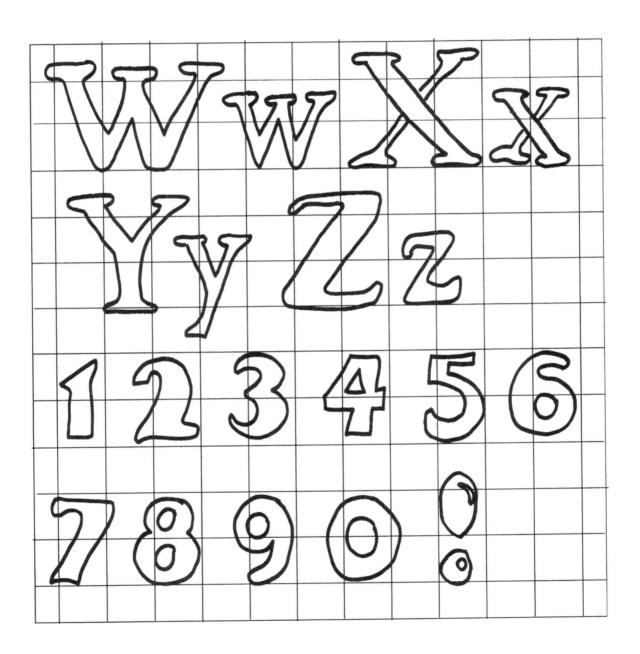

Computer Generated Alphabet

Aa Bb Cc Dd Ee
Ff Gg Hh Ii Jj Kk
Ll Mm Nn Oo Pp
Qq Rr Ss Tt Uu
Vv Ww Xx Yy Zz
1 2 3 4 5 6 7 8 9
10 (" , . ? ! : / * ")

Theme Lettering

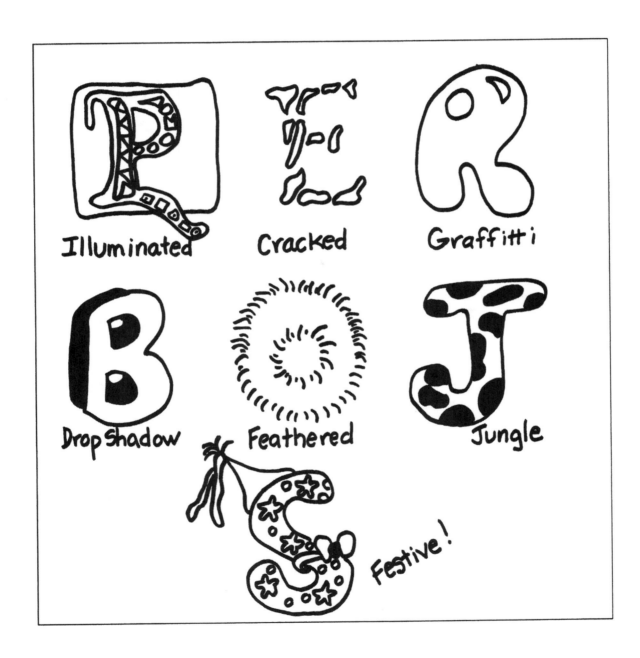

Illuminated

Cracked

Graffitti

Drop Shadow

Feathered

Jungle

Festive!

Practice Lettering Grid

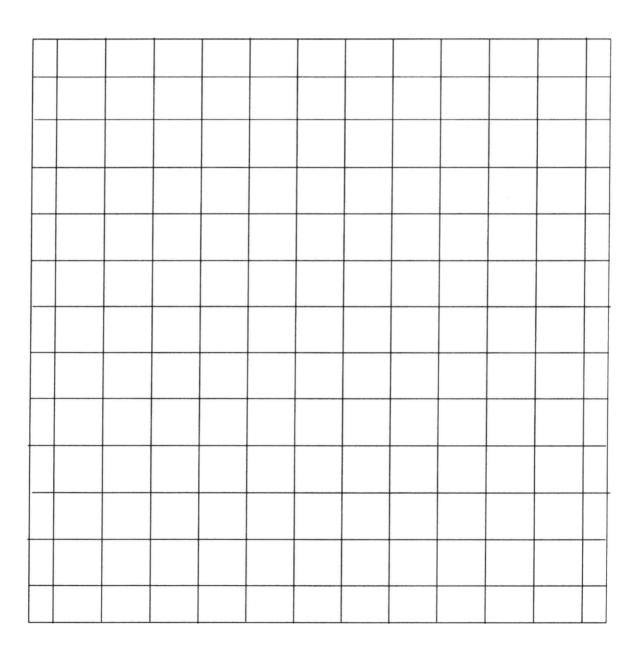

Practice Lettering Grid

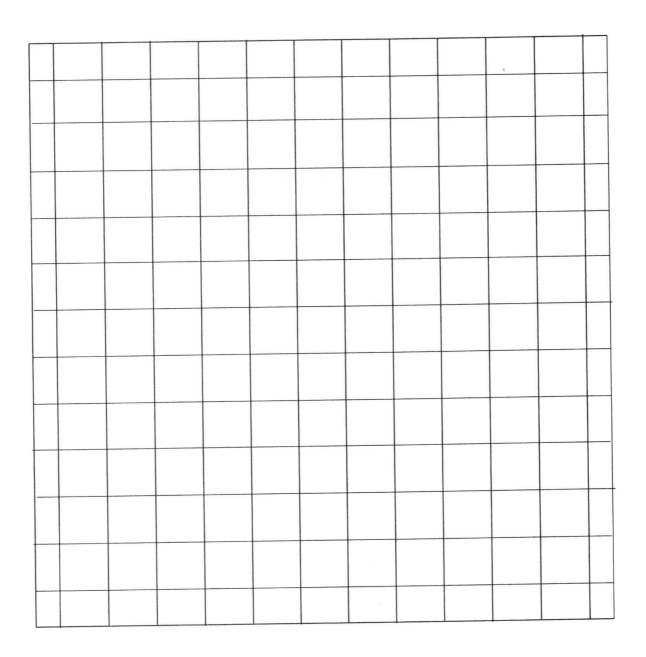

The Basics

Design

EZ Guide says: "Visual design can make plain, dull material interesting! Using the six EZ design steps along with your imagination, ingenuity and courage, your visuals will attract the reader's attention, hold it and transmit your message."

EZ GUIDE...

I can do this

The Six EZ Design Steps

1. Layout Decisions

When creating a visual, the first decision will be format selection. Choose between Portrait of Landscape

Portrait format is the layout this book is in, the majority of the space being vertical.

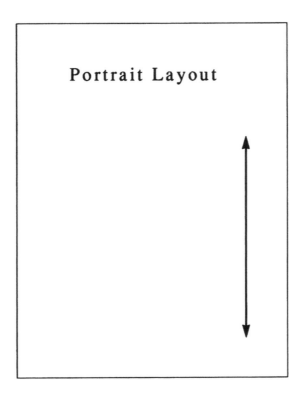

The landscape format turns the visual horizontally. This is a less frequently used format, but can be effective in regaining visual interest by changing the layout shape.

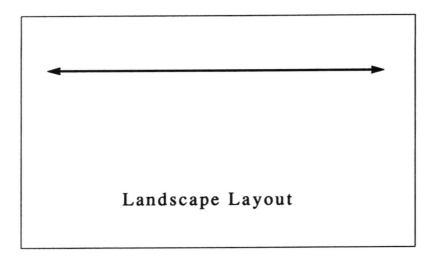

Landscape Layout

It is important to pick one format and create the majority of your visuals in that format. For visual unity in a total presentation, try to keep the design layout consistent.

Add an unexpected twist by hanging flip charts "crooked" (at left or right angles to the wall as if dancing) to gain attention.

2. **Border Design**

The next design step is choosing the type and style of border. If a series of visuals are related, use a border to unify the message. A simple rule for borders is to keep them plain and simple so as to not distract from the main message.

3. **Major Color Decision**

Select up to three major colors for the visual. Use a combination of activating, pacifying and neutralizing colors that are easily seen. Invest in a decorator's color wheel from a home store near you to choose colors that complement each other.

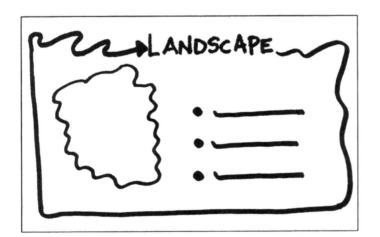

In the Western world, people look and read from left to right and top to bottom. Place important information at the top left of your visual and then attract the eye with lettering or graphics placed to the right. The eye's resting point will be towards the bottom left of the visual. This means once the eyes have finished reading, they will linger in the bottom left. Therefore, put something unique or interesting in the space

4. Thumbnail Sketch

Plan the best way to position the words and pictures on your visual. Draw thumbnail sketches with pencil on paper before starting. Include a strong title that can be recognized quickly. Look at the layout and ask yourself if it is pleasing to the eye or confusing. Your goal is to transmit your message clearly.

4. Thumbnail Sketch

5. **Lettering Decision**

Select the size and style of lettering that will make the greatest visual impact. Main titles or headings should be larger than sub-headings. Choose lettering that catches people's attention and is easy to read at a distance remembering that the more complicated styles do not necessarily work best.

6. **Graphic/Picture Decisions**

Finally, create your graphics. Look at their size in relation to the overall look. Are they too big or too small? Do they need to shift left, right, up or down? Copy examples of different balance elements from graphic design magazines and books.

Design Example

Design Checklist

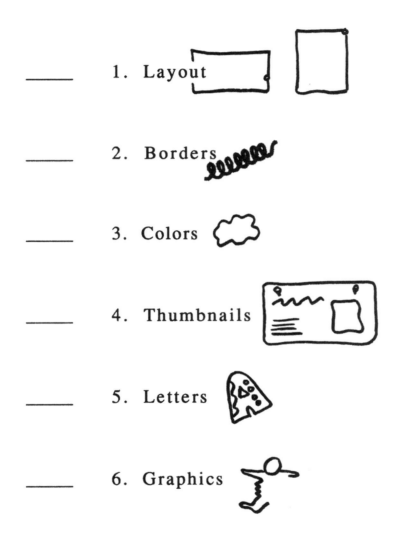

_____ 1. Layout

_____ 2. Borders

_____ 3. Colors

_____ 4. Thumbnails

_____ 5. Letters

_____ 6. Graphics

 # The Basics

 Images

EZ Guide says: "Make every effort to wed your graphic to your text! Graphics that are not related to the text presented can cause confusion!"

Graphic Images

Graphic images can be obtained or copied from books, clip art sources, children's coloring books or they can be drawn freehand.

There are five different graphic image categories

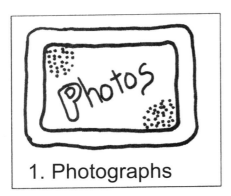

1. Photographs

The first type of image is an actual photograph. Film stores can duplicate, enlarge or downsize photographs for use with your visuals. When using photographs, check for copyright protection. If they are copywrited, write for permission before using the picture.

To create photos large enough to use on flip charts, take a normal size picture and enlarge it on a copy machine. Attach pictures to the chart paper with double sided or invisible tape. Add color by backing the picture with a colorful piece of construction paper. You can remove and reuse the picture when the charts wear out.

If you want to reproduce a graphic onto a flip chart from a transparency, simply project the image on the easel chart and trace the image onto the paper. Then add color, contrast and borders. Later, you can cut the picture out and reuse it on future charts.

When you decide to use photographs in your visual design, thumbnail sketch the layout first.

Thumbnail Sketch

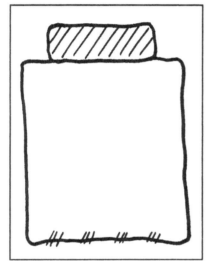

Layout: Portrait
Border Design
Title

Color Decision
Graphic Decision

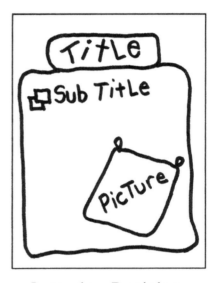

Lettering Decision

Experiment with a variety of colors, borders and lettering styles that match your photograph.

After finalizing your design, transfer your ideas to paper charts, transparencies or computer screens.

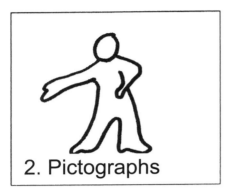

2. Pictographs

The second type of graphic image is a pictograph. Pictographs are simple line drawings that are easily recognized, but do not have the detail of the actual object. You will find step-by-step instructions for creating pictographs in the *Graphics* section (pages 90-92).

Some sample pictographs:

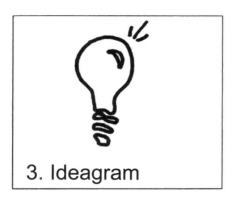

3. Ideagram

An ideagram represents an idea or thought that is conceptual in nature. Use a combination of simple lines and symbols to illustrate difficult concepts or to show emotions. Step-by-step ideagram instructions can be found in the *Graphics* section (pages 93-95).

Some sample ideagrams:

4. Iconotoons

The fourth type of graphic image is the iconotoon. This is a graphic presented in a fun and humorous way. To create iconotoons, simplify the picture into an icon and don't be afraid to exaggerate features for humorous effect or add a caption. Your will find step-by-step drawing panels for creating iconotoons in the **Graphics** section (pages 96-100).

Some sample iconotoons

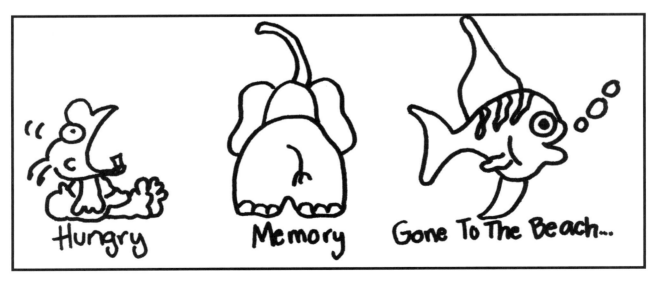

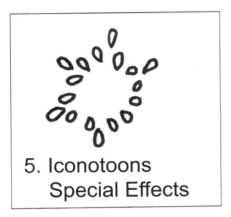

5. Iconotoons
   Special Effects

Add special effect marks to show action, fun and emotions around iconotoons. Your will find step-by-step drawing panels for creating iconotoons in the **Graphics** section (pages 96-100).

Some sample iconotoon special effects marks:

6. Starter Symbols

The last graphic image is a starter symbol. These symbols can separate, highlight and add interest to information. You can find creative starter symbols that appeal to you in the graphic design books and magazines. Starter symbols can be used as "bullets" or to identify items that belong together, just as we have done in each new section page in this chapter on The Basics.

Some sample starter symbols:

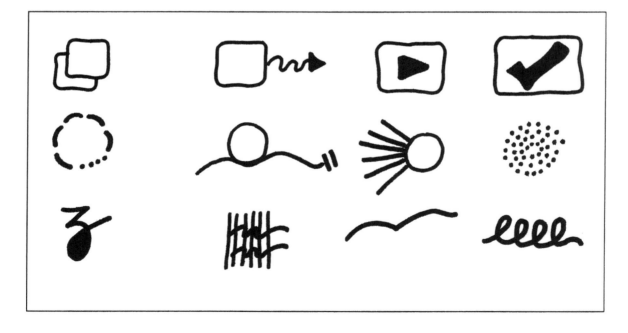

Step-by-step drawing panels and practice drawing areas for Pictographs, Ideagrams, and Iconotoons can be found the **Graphics** section.

Examples of how to use the different graphic images in a visual are in the **Ready Mades** section

The Graphics

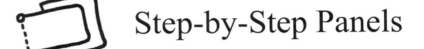

The Graphics

 Creating Shapes

EZ Guide says: "If you can draw ◯◯◯ 's, ▢▢▢ 's, △△△ 's and 〜〜〜 's -- you can turn words into pictures to create terrific graphics!"

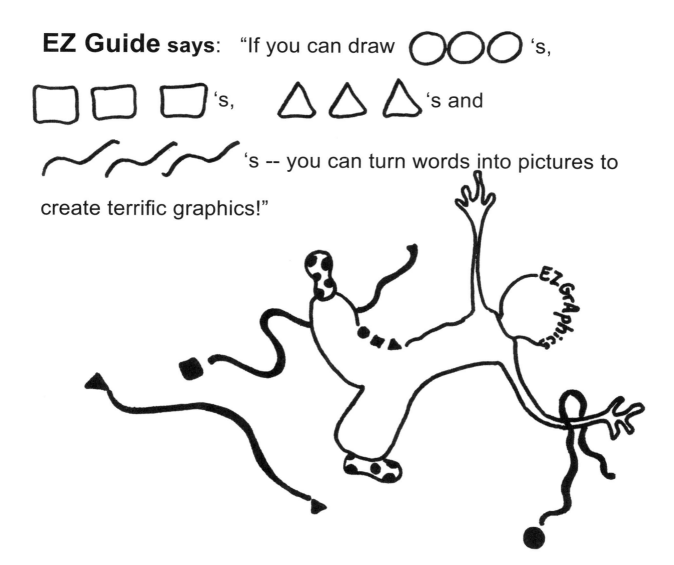

The Graphics: Creating Shapes

Whether your topic is detailed and complex or is difficult to conceptualize, your ability to communicate visually will greatly affect the amount of information your audience will understand and retain.

Simple hand drawn graphics can depict ideas, emotions and intangible concepts more easily and clearly than many spoken words.

Scientists and psychologists have found that the mind thinks in pictures - at times the pictures are three dimensional holographs, multi planed and in color. As a presenter, your job is to convey your content so the individuals attending will understand and remember your message. To accomplish this, your material must be presented in the way the mind thinks - in pictures.

The easiest way to illustrate concepts, ideas, theories, and complicated information is to draw a picture. This is nerve - racking for those of us who feel we are artistically challenged. People often say, "Oh, I can never draw a straight line!" Well, the good news is, it doesn't take straight lines to create the graphics you are about to learn. It only takes the ability to combine four basic, every day shapes that you are already used to drawing.

Start by drawing the following four shapes:

Then practice turning these shapes into graphics by copying the step-by-step panels as illustrated below:

Report :

Planet

Trees

Direction

Footsteps

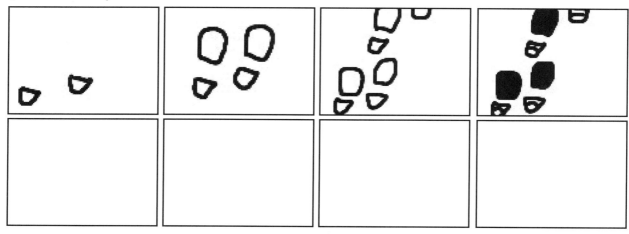

Temper

Cool Off

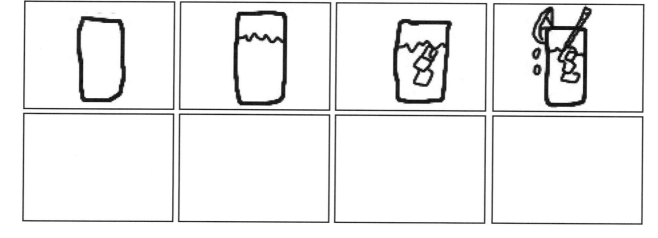

The Graphics

Step-by-Step Panels

EZ Guide says: "If you look at children's art in kindergarten, you'll see great examples of graphic communication. Kids are able to draw with uninhibited glee. Amazingly enough, it is easy to recover your natural drawing ability just by practicing and combining the basic shapes you are about to learn with these step by step panels."

Turning Words into Pictures: Step-by-Step

The following drawing panels are provided as guidelines to help you practice combining shapes to create Pictographs, Ideagrams and Iconotoons (as described in the Images section of the **Basics** chapter).

Copying is one way to learn how to draw. Notice how each graphic will begin with one of the basic foundation shapes and will continue to develop by adding additional shapes or lines to it.

Practice copying the shapes shown in each panel, then practice the various combinations on a sketch pad or in a sketchbook, until you can combine the shapes from memory.

Office Building

Pictograph Graphics: Step-by-Step

To draw pictographs (as described in the Images section of the **Basics** chapter), take an actual real life object and draw or copy it, reducing it to its basic elements.

You will begin by focusing on the basic shape, adding some simple line strokes and then adding your own creative details to complete the pictograph.

Since repetition and practice are the best ways to increase your drawing capabilities, use your broad point fiber tipped drawing pens to copy the pictographs shown in the panels provided below them, repeating each step slowly and deliberately.

Noteboo k

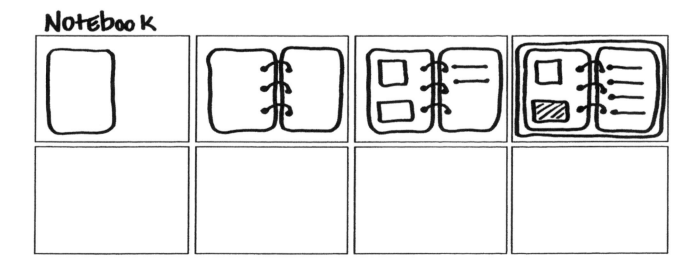

Person

Pencil

Flipchart

Balloons

Money

Presenter

Ideagram Graphics: Step-by-Step

Drawing an ideagram (as described in the Images section of the **Basics** chapter), is slightly more challenging, but by using the same basic shape foundation, you can design a graphic symbol or picture and create powerful images to illustrate your idea or concept.

Ideagrams are simple graphic images that represent a concept through an object. Usually, the graphic image is universal in nature and strongly associated with the idea, almost like a word.

For example, for the word love, the ideagram is

Idea

Productivity

Conflict

Rapport

UPWARDLY MobiLe

MoVING VeHicLe

Storm CLouds

Iconotoon Graphics: Step-by-Step

Iconotoon graphics are the most challenging to draw but often prove to be the most useful because they truly turn words into a picture.

To create an iconotoon (as described in the Images section of the **Basics** chapter) combine cartoon effects with icons to illustrate objects in a humorous way.

Iconotoon face drawings are possibly the easiest and best way to illustrate emotions. Your main concern is to make sure your iconotoons are immediately understandable and that you will be able to draw them quickly and easily in front of your audience!

Hungry

Whew!

Gone Fishin'

Timer

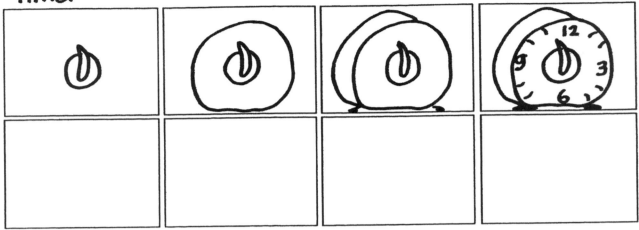

Reading

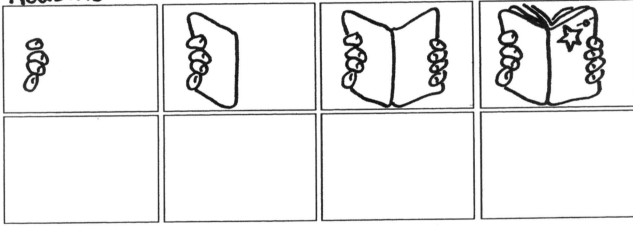

Memory

Calculate

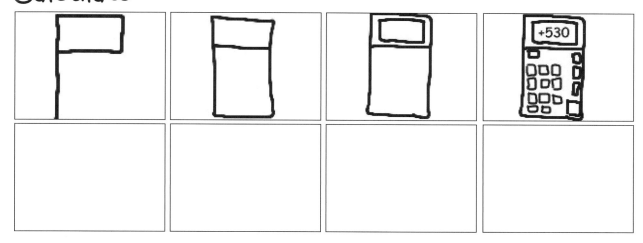

Jump

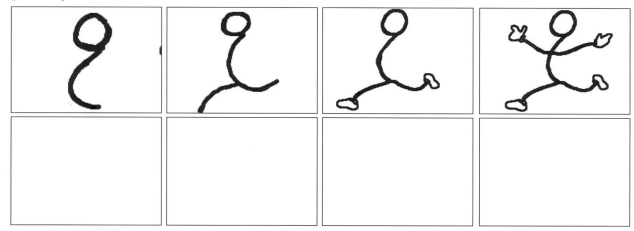

Fish

Enlighten

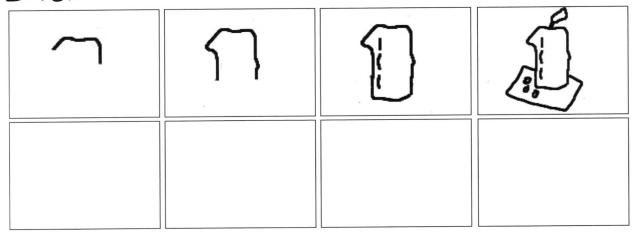

Coffee Break

First

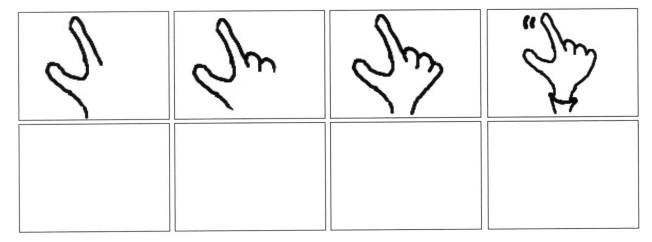

The Graphics

 Graphic Language Library

EZ Guide says: "Because the mind thinks in pictures, your message will be so much more memorable if you can demonstrate your point by drawing those pictures quickly, easily and effortlessly!"

Creating Graphic Language

By using different combinations of lines, squares, circles, angles and cartooning effects, you can create your own graphic language library.

Many ideagrams and iconotoons (see the **Graphics** chapter, Step-by-Step section) transfer easily into an instantly recognized graphic language. Your aim is to find easy and quick to draw pictures that relate directly to your concept or idea. We have provided some of our favorite graphic language symbols.

You'll find an area at the end of this section that you can use to practice our favorites and begin to create and add some of your own. You can even add our favorites to your computer presentations by using the CD-ROM provided with this book. All you need to do is find the picture you want, and then locate the file on the CD-ROM (file names use the name provided in the Graphic Library). Insert it into your presentation software as you would clip art.

ACTION

AiRMAiL

All THAT JAZZ

ANATOMY

ANNOUNCING

ARTISTIC

BALANCE

BOOK BUDDY

BZ AS A BEE

CARE

CHARMING

CONTINUOUS

CONVERSATION

COMFORT

COMMUNICATION

COUNSEL

DIALOGUE

DIRECTION

FLYIN' HIGH

FRESH PAINT

FUN

GENERATE

GRAPH MAN

HELP!

HIGH FIVE

LEADERSHIP

LEAP

MAIL

MANAGEMENT

MEMORABLE

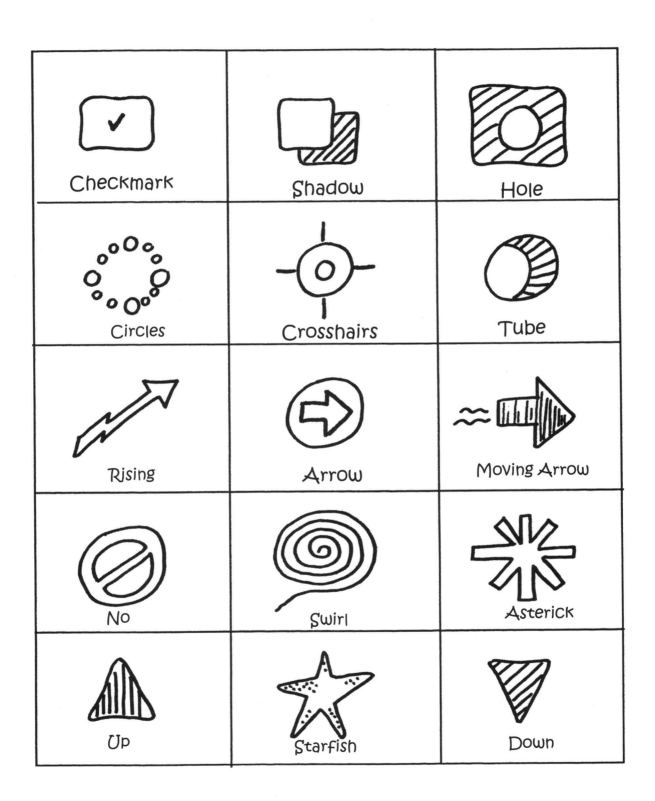

Checkmark	Shadow	Hole
Circles	Crosshairs	Tube
Rising	Arrow	Moving Arrow
No	Swirl	Asterick
Up	Starfish	Down

Mad as a Hornet

Make Tracks

Martian

Nightfall

Oh No!

On Thin Ice

One Full Minute

Oops

Ouch

Peace

Procedures

Quiet

Ready!

Robotics

Say What?

The Graphics

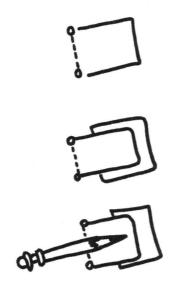

The VIG Page

VIG = Very Important Graphic

EZ Guide says: "Use the **VIG** page tips about visual communication to inspire you to continue your efforts to reignite your natural design and drawing talents."

The VIG (Very Important Graphic) Page!

At intervals in your class, include a WOW idea like this **VIG** page is used in this book to renew interest and reignite the viewer's brain so it can absorb more information. Get their attention with a surprise picture.

Do something unexpected in your visual. Include a surprise graphic, hide a clue, utilize an unusual bright color. This **VIG** page is an example. It is unusual to see a fish jump off a page!

If your message and information is detailed or complex, you will want to refocus your audience every so often with an interesting or unusual graphic so they are not lulled off to sleep.

Test yourself by looking for basic shapes and lines in every graphic and artwork example you encounter in everyday life. Then, copy the graphic into your sketch book for future use.

Look for VIG ideas on the CD-ROM!

VIG tips you have discovered and plan to use!

The Quick and Easy Ideas

 Visual Communication

 10 Minute Visual Ideas

 20 Minute Visual Ideas

 30+ Minute Visual Ideas

The Quick and Easy Ideas

Visual Communication

EZ Guide says: "Try to integrate as many different visual activities and approaches as you can!"

Visual Communication

Quick and Easy visual ideas are compiled from the ideas shared by corporate trainers, professional speakers and educators from the United States and Canada. We are ever so grateful to all of the individuals who have been so generous in sharing their creative thoughts.

Visual communication has the advantage of being understood faster and easier than the written word.

Since your audience can actually see ideas and solutions, they will absorb and retain visual information at an accelerated rate.

Visual Communication

Compare  to **"No Pedestrians Allowed"**

The visual difference emphasizes how easy it is to increase understanding and comprehension by using quick, easy to grasp graphics. When people connect these visual communications to the presented information, the learning process becomes fun and successful.

Communicating visually is like athletics: if you don't practice, your creative abilities you will get flabby and out of shape. You can stimulate your creativity by:

    *Using versatility and simplicity as your creative guideline
    *Trying one new idea every time you create a new visual
    *Experimenting with new styles and graphics
    *Keeping visuals uncluttered, with facts displayed clearly
    *Creating large and easy to read titles and headings
    *Using up to three colors on your visuals
    *Making diagrams and pictures relevant to your message
    *Presenting your information briefly
    *Observing visuals everywhere to find new ideas

The Quick and Easy Ideas

10 Minute Visual Ideas

EZ Guide **says**: "Here are some visual ideas and activities that only take 10, 20, or 30+ minutes to prepare.

Visual Brainstorming

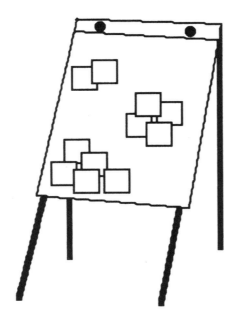

An easy way to brainstorm visually is to invite group members to write their ideas on Post-It Notes. Then, the group goes round robin, placing one Post-It Note on a flip chart or a white board at a time.

Cluster Post-Its with similar ideas together. As the session continues, the Post-It Note ideas are movable, so that strategies and team planning can occur and ideas and action issues can be recorded and then assigned to different teams or group members.

Agenda Self Adhesive Note Markers

Focusing everyone's attention on the day's agenda is easy with this self adhesive note idea.

Use a self adhesive note with a theme graphic as a place marker on the agenda. As an example, if teaching a computer course, draw a mouse on the self adhesive note and place it alongside the session topic you are about to start or have just completed.

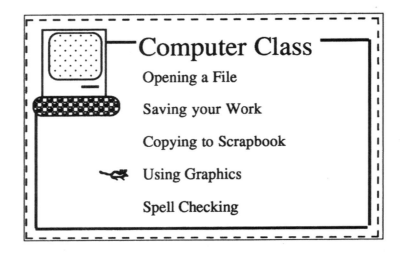

The agenda should be visible to the entire room. Explain that a self adhesive note place marker will mark the agenda items as information is covered. To recall what content has been covered, attendees can glance at the agenda displayed throughout the day. This also allows those who have drifted away from the lesson to quickly assess where the class is.

Creating Self Adhesive Note Pointers

Cut a variety of pointer shapes and arrows out of self adhesive notes. The shapes will stick wherever needed on any type of visual, and are moveable, and reusable.

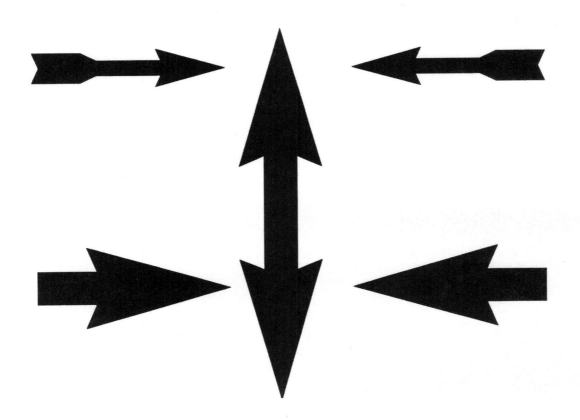

Giant Pointers

Giant pointers can highlight a part of you message by using an actual object to gain the attention of your participants.   You might want to create an unusual chart pointer yourself. To create this prop, obtain a winter glove and stuff it with fiberfill, sewing it closed. Attach it to a stick or dowel at the base of the glove and use it as a super sized pointer for your flipchart.

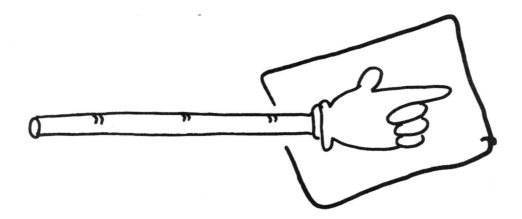

You can also place jewelry such as an old ring or a childen's plastic watch on the hand for added interest. Use different colors and types of gloves and change pointers to see who is watching and listening over long training classes.

Tape Flag Identifiers

The **3M** company makes Post-It Tape Flags in a variety of sizes and colors. To look more professional and prepared in your presentation, the flags can be used to reference, color code and easily access your visual charts.

The colored areas of the Tape Flags can be labeled with a permanent marker or ball point pen. Arrange the tape flags in a staggered fashion down the side of flip charts to identify them as you create and draw them.

You can avoid stopping and searching for a chart that is already prepared.

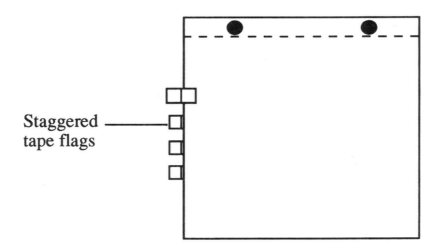

Staggered tape flags

Electronic Visuals

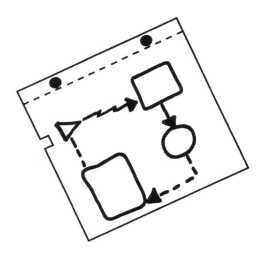

An electronic white board allows you to create visuals on a large white board and then provide your audience with instant copies of what you have drawn. A small copy-like machine located at the bottom of the easel provides the copies instantly. What a great time saver for distributing notes immediately rather than copying, typing and distributing them following the meeting. Alternatively, if you have loaded your visuals into your computer, just print them out as handouts.

The Quick and Easy Ideas

20 Minute Visual Ideas

EZ Guide says: "The more ways you are open to doing new things, the easier it will be for you to communicate your message and ideas."

A Visual Parking Lot

During meetings or in educational settings, questions and issues come up that the facilitator may want to put on hold until later. One way to deal with this is to use a visual known as a "Parking Lot."

Use a clean chart paper, draw a graphic that looks like a parking lot with spaces drawn for each "car." Place Post-It Notes (regular or car-shaped) within reach of participants. If an issue or questions comes up, ask the person who raised it to write it down on a Post-It and place it in a space on the visual parking lot. Before the session is over, deal with all the questions and issues on the chart inviting participants to join in answering the questions.

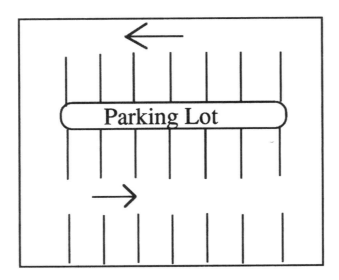

Visual Form Completion

When working and teaching the completion of new forms, this simple filp chart idea is terrific!

First, create a transparency of the form to be learned. Project the form on a clean easel chart so the entire form is visible. Use the image to demonstrate how to fill in the sample forms.

Then provide a fresh sheet for teams to practice on by turning the filled-in, used chart over the back of the easel.

Visual 3-D Objects

A simple and high impact visual idea is to use actual physical objects attached to your charts or white board or placed on top of your transparencies. Picking an object that is related to the content can make a dramatic attention-getting point.

Sample 3-D Objects

Idea	Represented By
Agenda Marker	Plastic hand
Attention to Detail	Eyeglasses, sunglasses
Break Time	Empty soft drink can
Infection Control	A surgical plastic glove

Select objects such as an actual machine part or a piece of equipment. This is quicker and easier than freehand drawing a picture of the item.

Chart papers still attached to the easel pad provide a more stable surface than single charts attached to the wall. For best results, use **Handi-Tak** (reusable adhesive) or **3M** masking tape #232 or #234 when attaching the 3-D objects to the wall.

Cover Up Agenda Markers

Create a visual of your course agenda, placing check marks next to each agenda item. If the visual is a poster, cover the check marks with self adhesive notes. Use small physical objects to cover the check marks on transparencies. As modules of the course are completed, remove the objects or self adhesive notes so the check marks become visible. Removing the cover ups allows the visual agenda to be used again and again.

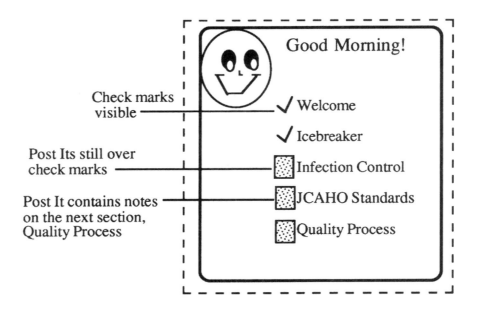

Cover up self adhesive notes can also serve as presentation notes by placing key content points on them. As the self adhesive notes are removed, presentation of the next content item can be given without obvious notes.

Visual Dueling Activity

Place one easel at
the front of the room.

Invite both a right and a left-handed scribe to record ideas learned in
the sessions. This will allow each person to stand on a different side
of the easel so that he or she can quickly record ideas and allow the
group to see the charts as the ideas are recorded.

This activity encourages the quick free flow of ideas because, visually,
it looks as if the scribes are racing each other to record the most ideas.
It also frees the presenter to act as facilitator, encouraging and guiding
group's memory.

Visual Keyhole Cutouts

Visuals that use photographs, complex graphics or hand drawn pieces of artwork can be created quickly and easily by using a Quick & Easy 20 minute idea known as a keyhole cutout. A graphic is placed under clean, fresh piece of chart paper and a keyhole cutout opening is made with a razor like tool (a coupon cutter or artists clip it) to allow the picture to show through.

How to Create a Keyhole:

On one of the last pages of a PaperChart pad, attach a picture or graphic. Use double stick tape or masking tape loops to attach the picture to the PaperChart so the tape will not show.

Pull one to seven pages down over the picture. Using your cutting tool, cut out the paper laying directly on top of the picture, so that it shows through all of the pages.

If using lined or graphed chart paper, it will be easy to cut an even box out around the picture. If using plain, newsprint paper, draw curved lines with rounded edges around the image and follow this with your cutting tool.

Cutting the keyhole through several sheets of clean paper allows for recording spontaneous audience input on the top page. When that page is full, flip it over and continue recording on the next page. The picture stays visible throughout the turning of the pages because the keyhole cutout allows it to be seen no matter which page is being written on. Continue to turn and record on a fresh page all the way down to the picture.

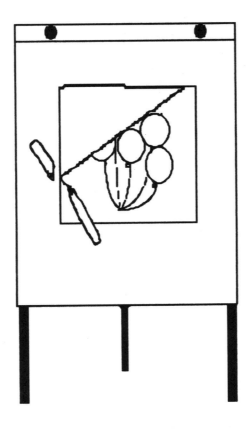

A quick and easy tip that will increase the life of the reusable keyhole artwork, graphic or photograph is to cover them with a frame of thick, clear adhesive tape or **3M** masking tape. This will prevent destroying the artwork when removing it from the chart paper. New tape can be attached easily to the frame when ready to be used again.

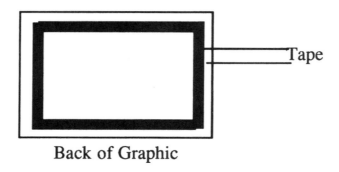

Back of Graphic

For the next session, reuse the same artwork, pull two to seven blank chart pages down over it and cut out a new keyhole. This will allow reuse of the artwork, picture or graphic indefinitely.

Practice keyhole cutout:

Visual Keyhole Cutouts

Use freehand artwork, photographs, clip art, computer graphics, content related items, anything that will visually portray your message.

The Quick and Easy Ideas

30+ Minute Visual Ideas

EZ Guide says: "Allow your audience time for reading, retention and note taking before removing your visuals."

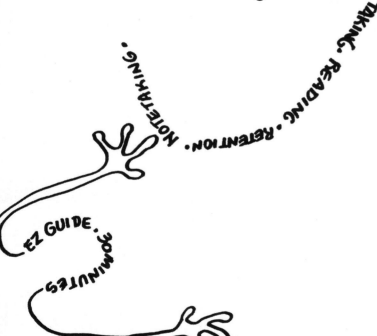

Magic Paper Letters

This idea involves a series of cut out visual paper letters that are used together in a presentation. Select a theme word directly related to the content message and make it into a point of interest in the design of the visual.

In the top left hand corner of the visual (or even in the border), place one paper letter per chart and present the charts in the order that will spell the selected word.

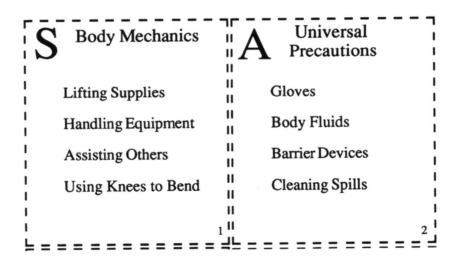

Continue to present the information without mentioning the letter placed in the corner. When someone notices the letters and deciphers the word, you can reward him or her.

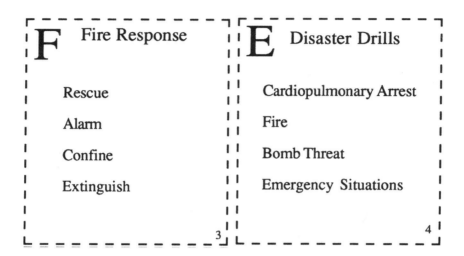

At the end of your presentation, if the letters or word go unnoticed, ask participants if they can see anything unusual about the visual. Go to the first chart and direct their attention to the lettered area. Turn the pages so that everyone can see all of the letters. Conclude by asking them how this "word" relates to the content of the day.

T Environment

Accidents

Electrical Cords

Equipment

Spills

5

Y Personal

Parking

Off Campus Site

Psychiatric

6

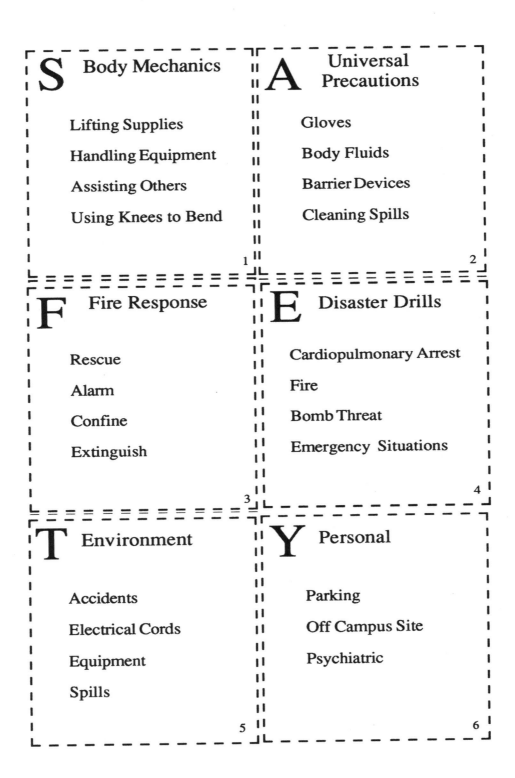

S Body Mechanics

Lifting Supplies

Handling Equipment

Assisting Others

Using Knees to Bend

1

A Universal Precautions

Gloves

Body Fluids

Barrier Devices

Cleaning Spills

2

F Fire Response

Rescue

Alarm

Confine

Extinguish

3

E Disaster Drills

Cardiopulmonary Arrest

Fire

Bomb Threat

Emergency Situations

4

T Environment

Accidents

Electrical Cords

Equipment

Spills

5

Y Personal

Parking

Off Campus Site

Psychiatric

6

Whole Brain Grids

This visual communication technique organizes or "chunks" visual information into window-like boxes which serve as a memory cue. The technique taps into the spatial aspects of retention and is based on the concept that short term memory can retain seven items at a time, plus or minus two. The maximum recommended number of grids is nine.

Advanced preparation time is needed, but visual whole brain grids are easy to make and highly reusable.

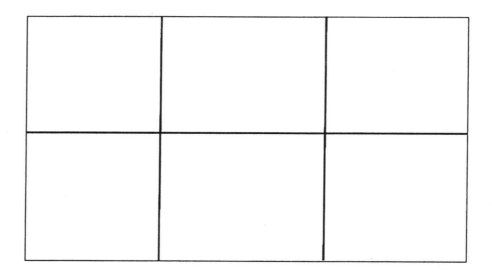

The concept is shown in visual format, one element at a time, in each grid box. As the concept is shown, an auditory explanation is given that ties the picture to the idea. Each box builds on the previous information shown, until all of the boxes are filled in. By involving your audience's visual and auditory senses, you have created a powerful memory tool.

A Whole Brain Grid Activity

An example of a Whole Brain Grid used to teach the adult Heimlich maneuver to lay persons according to the American Heart Association standards is shown below. The pictures in each square key the memory to important points.

The presenter can either use a copy of computer generated graphics or freehand draw the figures into each of the window boxes. Each step is followed by an explanation.

The audience is asked to record a brief note or caption and draw a copy of the Whole Brain Grid boxes as each step is presented. Periodically, to reinforce learning, ask the participants to revisit the boxes they have drawn and restate the explanations to themselves.

Adult Heimlich Maneuver Whole Brain Grid

There are nine steps taught in the order that the grid boxes are laid out. The boxes are read from top left to top right, continuing on to the middle row, from left to right and finishing with the bottom row, from left to right.

Step 1:

In the top left corner, suspect person is choking, face is red, hands may be up around the throat, tongue is hanging out.

Step 2:

The top middle box with the question mark represents the rescuer asking the choking victim, "Are you choking?"

Step 3:

The top right hand box represents the universal symbol, SOS, with the rescuer saying to the victim, "I can help you!"

Step 4:

The center row left box has a pair of arms coming together. This represents the rescuer standing behind the choking person, placing his or her arms around and under the victim's arms.

Adult Heimlich Maneuver Whole Brain Grid

Step 5:
   The center row middle box represents the rescuer making a special fist, placing the thumb inside of the fist.

Step 6:
   The center row right box represents the rescuer placing the special fist where **X** marks the spot, below the ribs and above the waist.

Step 7:
   The bottom row left box is a picture of a spinning top representing the rescuer placing their non-dominant hand on top of the already laced special fist.

Step 8:
   The bottom row center box is an upward pointing arrow representing the rescuer pulling up and back with both hands in order to dislodge the obstruction.

Adult Heimlich Maneuver Whole Brain Grid

Step 9:

The bottom row right box represents success in dislodging the obstruction with a smiling face. The stick figure lying down represents waiting for paramedics if the victim has passed out or continuing the Heimlich maneuver until the person is no longer choking.

After the Whole Brain Grid boxes have been taught and the sequenced pictures recorded, ask participants what each picture represents. They will remember most of the meanings, even if they were totally unfamiliar with the Heimlich maneuver.

To help cement retention of the nine steps and the pictures of the Heimlich Maneuver, switch to an empty whole brain grid and place your hand in any box. Ask learners what picture should appear in each of the boxes, and the meaning of each box. For maximum comprehension and retention, have the whole group shout out the answers as you move around the blank Whole Brain Grid squares.

Whole Brain Grids

The purpose for creating visuals in this manner is to present a process that encourages high retention. Any other sequential process can be easily adapted to this format. Key concepts that are not sequential can also be adapted in this way as long as the pictures used in the grid boxes are easy to recognize and remember.

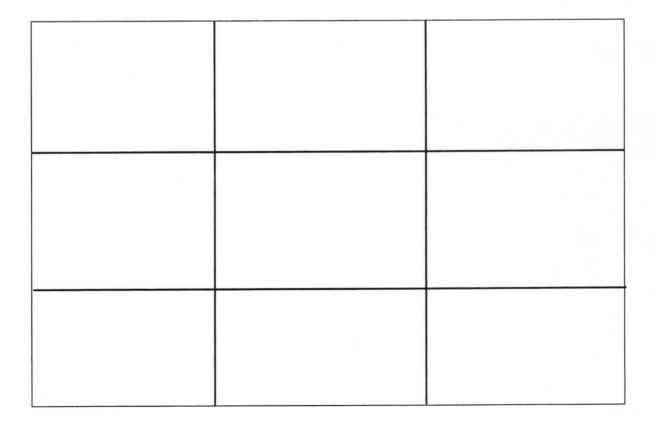

Whole Brain Grid

A Master Copy

PosterPrinter Visuals

Visuals can be created by using a machine offered by Varitronics called the PosterPrinter Plus. This machine allows you to insert letter-sized originals - text, graphics, or both - and turn the original into a 23" x 30" poster sized chart. You can also switch the PosterPrinter to a double size setting and enlarge the same original to a 45" x 35" poster.

PosterLynx, a program available for PC's and Macs, allows you to print presentation graphs, posters, flip charts and banners. The special banner kit, included with the PosterPrinter, provides ready-to-use agendas, announcements, welcome graphics and letters/number originals formats.

Original photographs, schematics and flowcharts can also be used to create visuals with the PosterPrinter because of the machine's high resolution capabilities. Reverse imaging is available and a variety of different colored posters can be created using different colored printer paper rolls.

The Ready Made Visuals

 Ready Made, Ready to Go

 5 Minute Quick Draw

 10 Minute Fast Draw

 15+ Minute Ready Mades

The Ready Made Visuals

Ready Made, Ready to Go

EZ Guide says: "Oh, what a treat! Here you'll find time-saving and copy-ready graphic ideas. Whether you have plenty of time to prepare your visuals in advance, or just 5 minutes to sketch or finish your computer presentation before you speak, use this section of the book to help you generate ideas."

The Ready Made Visuals on the CD-ROM

Whether you are new or experienced at the art of creating visuals, use all of the following Ready Made examples to help you generate artistic ideas, no matter what the medium.

 Use the file pages on the CD-ROM to design, print or sketch visual layouts.

 Copy, enlarge and trace any of the graphics. After selecting some of the graphics, rearrange and mix and match them to create new visuals.

 Import a sample visual into your computer presentation, and liven things up. Just find the picture file in the respective chapter directory folder of the accompanying CD-ROM. Then find the page number of your desired Ready Made as the filename and import it.

 Copy the Ready Made example onto a transparency and project it onto an easel chart so the basic layout design and images can be traced onto flip chart paper.

 Once you have copied, traced, imported, or drawn your visual, laminate it for durability and indefinite use.

The Ready Made Visuals

 5 Minute Quick Draw

EZ Guide **says**: "Here are some easy-to copy visual ideas that only take 3 to 5 minutes to reproduce, import or draw!"

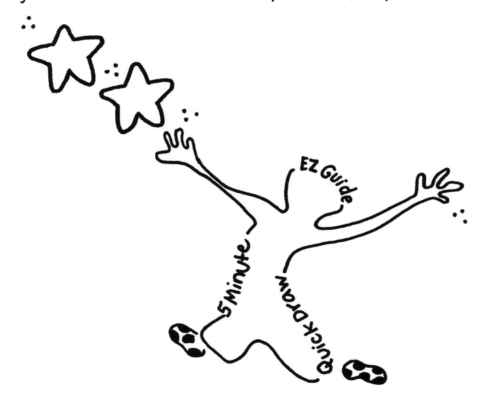

The Ready Made Visuals

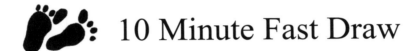 10 Minute Fast Draw

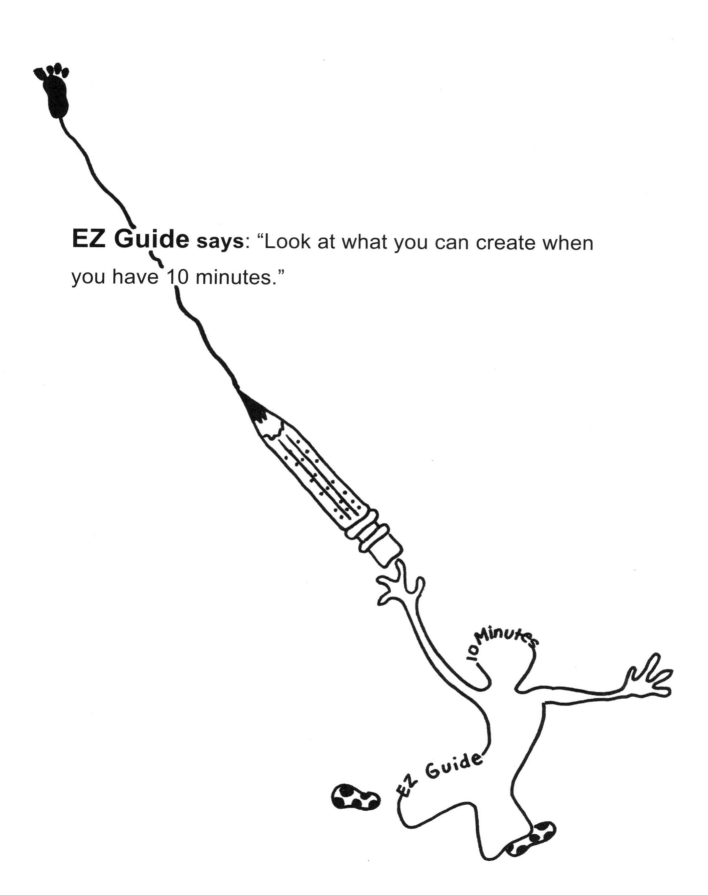

EZ Guide **says**: "Look at what you can create when you have 10 minutes."

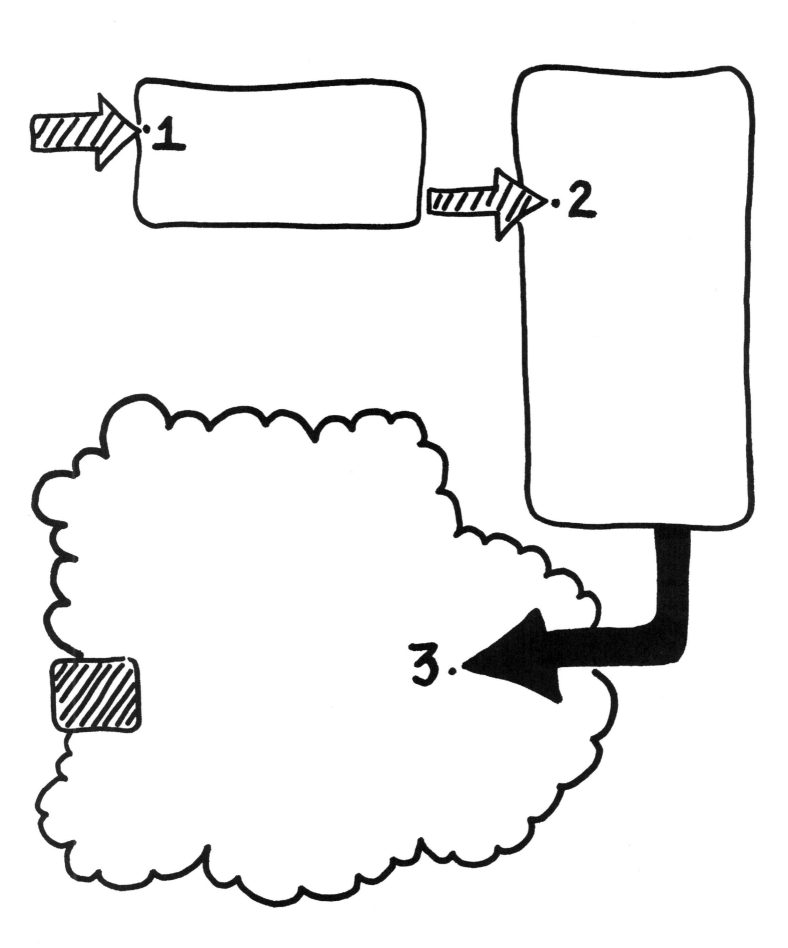

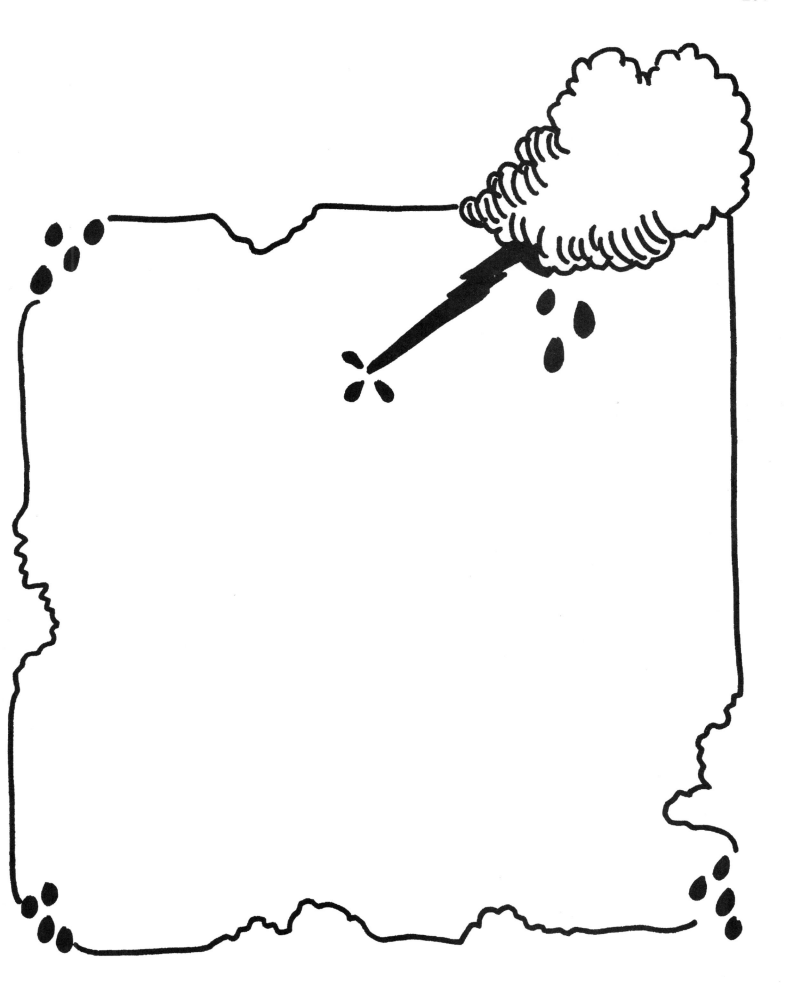

The Ready Made Visuals

15+ Minute Ready Mades

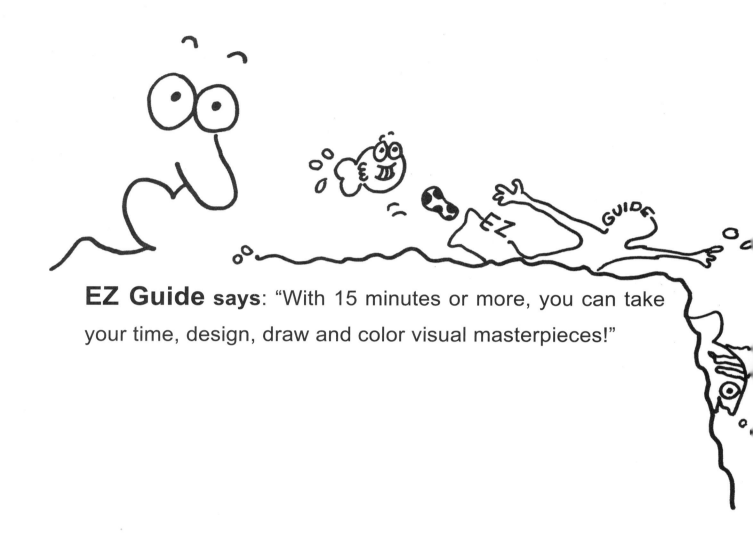

EZ Guide says: "With 15 minutes or more, you can take your time, design, draw and color visual masterpieces!"

whew oh boy wow
oh boy oh boy oh boy whew
whew
whew
whew oh whew boy oh boy

OK TO GO

Fishin...

Final Thoughts

be free enjoy your moods
believe in yourself
celebrate your talent
draw every single chance you get
play eat cookies and ice cream
hug laugh make
friends with children
take couch time give drawing
supply gifts seek out
artistically challenged artists
and admire their
artwork

This book is designed to provide you with easy-to-draw graphics and visual ideas and examples that you can trace, copy, import, or reproduce very quickly.

As you practice creating your visuals, try including:

- humorous graphics
    - different color combinations
        - outrageous cartoon characters
            - unexpected contrasts --
                tiny/huge
                light/dark
                smooth/jagged

Through our travels and research, we discovered that many presenters want to design and create visuals that vividly show what they are trying to say and that intrigue and fascinate their audiences. We hope our book will start you on a journey into visual thinking and communication.

Wishing you an abundance of imagination, ingenuity, courage and fun!

Lori Backer   **Michele Deck**

The Resources

Lori and Michele can custom design permanent visual sets tailored to your requirements. They are also available to conduct EZ Graphic Workshops.

Contact:

Tool Thyme for Trainers
EM: gamesinc4@aol.com
504.887.5558
www.tool-trainers.com

The Resources

Newest References:

Blitz, B. **The Fun Book of Cartoon Faces**, Philadelphia: Running Press, 1999.

Blitz, B. **The Fun Book of Cartoon People**, Philadelphia: Running Press, 1999.

Blitz, B. **The Big Book of Cartooning**, Philadelphia: Running Press, 1998.

Burgess, A., **The Do It Yourself Lettering Book**, Memphis: Troll Assoc., 1998.

Cameron, J. **The Artist's Way: A Spiritual Path to Higher Creativity**, Rutherford: Penguin Putnam, Inc., 2002.

Glasbergen, R. Toons!: **How to Draw Wild and Lively Characters for All Kinds of Cartoons**, Cincinnati: North Light Books, 1997.

Margulies, N. **Mapping Inner Space**, Tucson: Zephyr Press, 2002.

Millbower, L and Yager, D. **Cartoons for Trainers**, Sterling: Stylus Publishing, 2002.

Striker, S., Kimmel, E., **The Second Anti Coloring Book: Creative Activities for Ages 6 and Up**, New York: Owl Books, 2001.

Classic References:

Blitz, B. **Blitz Cartooning Kit**, Philadelphia: Running Press, 1991.

Brandt, R. **Flip Charts**, Richmond: Brandt Management Group, 1987.

Emberly, E. **Drawing Book of Faces**, Boston: Little, Brown and Company, 1992.

Hart, C. **Making Funny Faces**, New York: Watson-Guptill Publications, 1992.

Liungman, C. G., **Dictionary of Symbols**, New York: W.W. Norton, 1994.

SARK, **A Creative Companion: How to Free Your Creative Spirit**, Berkeley: Celestial Arts, 1991.

Tatchell, J., **How to Draw Cartoons and Caricatures**, St Petersburg: EDC Publications, 1988.

Tatchell, J., **How to Draw Lettering**, St Petersburg: EDC Publications, 1993.

White, J. **Graphic Idea Notebook**, Gloucester: Rockport Publishers, Inc, 1991.

About The Authors

Michele Deck

an internationally renown presenter, author, nurse, and educator is the co-founder, President and Chief Executive Officer of G.A.M.E.S., a company that specializes in adult learning and interactive teaching methods and provides seminars for any organization, nationally and internationally.

She is also CEO of Tool Thyme for Trainers, a company she founded that supplies the most innovative and creative presentation tools available to educators worldwide. Her extensive travels have resulted in thousands of people gaining valuable expertise in adult education and training, from Australia to Scotland, Canada to Taiwan.

Michele consistently receives high evaluations due to her fun, informative, and idea filled sessions. She has facilitated over 700 learning sessions on many and various topics.

She has won the prestigious "Excellence in Nursing" award has also been selected as a "Great 100 Nurse in Louisiana" and was elected to Sigma Theta Tau National Nursing Honor Society. She was named the recipient of the prestigious Belinda Puetz award by the National Nursing Staff Development Organization in 2000. She is the author of a thrice yearly column in the National Nursing Staff Development's professional journal.

Her seven latest books: Instant Teaching Tools For Healthcare Educators, Presenter's Survival Kit: It's A Jungle Out There! , Getting Adults Motivated, Enthusiastic and Satisfied, Volume One and Two The Presenter's E-Z Graphics Kit, More Instant Teaching Tools For Healthcare Educators and Live To Train Another Day. She has been a contributing author to the Joint Commission Guide to Staff Education and Conversations in Nursing Professional Development.

Some of Michele's clients include Dun and Bradstreet, Hibernia National Bank,Bayley and Bender, Bank One,United Parcel Service, Haagen Daz Ice Cream, Informix, United States Coast Guard Academy, Abbott Labs, Eli Lilly, Boston Pizza, Southern Nuclear, Oxford Shirt Company, Southwest Airlines, Lifetouch Photography,

Michele's healthcare clients include American Association of Critical Care Nurses, Association of Operating Room Nurses, National Association of Orthopedic Nurses, American Association of Office Nurses, Emergency Nurses Association, American Association of Occupational Health Nurses, American Association of Diabetes Educators, Sanofi Pharmaceuticals, Lovelace Health Services, SCA Hygiene Products, Louisiana Department of Health and Hospitals, Naval School of Health Sciences, and Florida Hospital.

Lori Backer

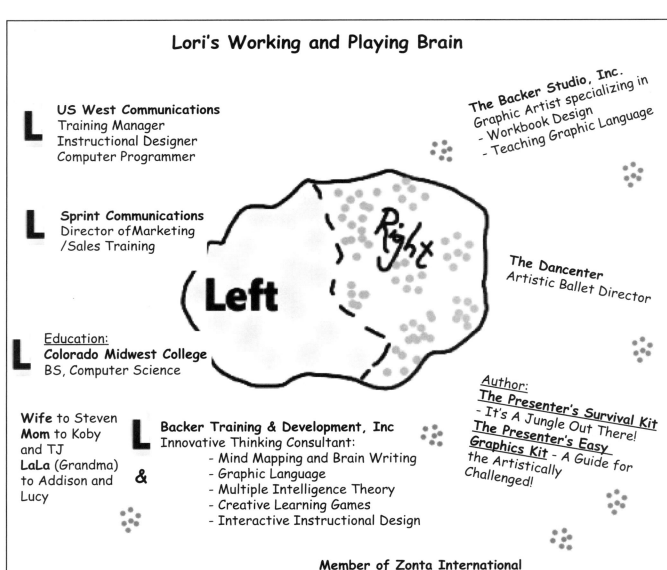

Lori's Working and Playing Brain

L US West Communications
Training Manager
Instructional Designer
Computer Programmer

L Sprint Communications
Director of Marketing
/Sales Training

L Education:
Colorado Midwest College
BS, Computer Science

Wife to Steven
Mom to Koby
and TJ
LaLa (Grandma)
to Addison and
Lucy

&

L Backer Training & Development, Inc
Innovative Thinking Consultant:
- Mind Mapping and Brain Writing
- Graphic Language
- Multiple Intelligence Theory
- Creative Learning Games
- Interactive Instructional Design

The Backer Studio, Inc.
Graphic Artist specializing in
- Workbook Design
- Teaching Graphic Language

The Dancenter
Artistic Ballet Director

Author:
The Presenter's Survival Kit
- It's A Jungle Out There!
The Presenter's Easy Graphics Kit - A Guide for
the Artistically
Challenged!

Member of Zonta International